Workbook

For

Phil Stutz and Barry Michels'

The Tools

Smart Reads

Note to readers:
This is an unofficial workbook for Phil Stutz
and Barry Michels' "The Tools: 5 Tools to
Help You Find Courage, Creativity, and
Willpower--and Inspire You to Live Life in
Forward Motion" designed to enrich your
reading experience. The original book can
be purchased on Amazon.

Download Your Free Gift

As a way to say "Thank You" for being a fan of our series, I've included a free gift for you:

Brain Health: How to Nurture and Nourish Your Brain For Top Performance

Go to www.smart-reads.com to get your FREE book.

The Smart Reads Team

Table of Contents

How To Use This Book

This workbook is designed to help you have a deeper understanding of Phil Stutz and Barry Michels' book. In order to get the most out of the book and apply the concepts, do the following.

1) Read the chapter summaries in this book to get an overview or "big picture" understanding of the book.

2) Read Phil Stutz and Barry Michels' original work. The details of the book will be easier to understand once you grasp the big picture.

3) Once you understand the core concepts, start working through the exercises in this workbook.

4) To assist you with applying the main concepts, the following exercises are present.

Key Takeaways: Main key points to help you understand the most important topics.

Reflective Questions: These questions guide you to reflect on your own experiences and figure out what needs to be done to change your life. Write your thoughts in the lines present in this workbook.

Action Step: Practical steps are discussed to lead you to take action so you can improve your life.

You must **THINK** before doing. This is how you can make changes to lead a new life.

Overview of *The Tools – 5 Tools to Help You Find Courage, Creativity, and Willpower*

Psychiatrist Phil Stutz and psychotherapist Barry Michels have taken a revolutionary forward-looking approach to face daily challenges that could be hindering your life improvement. The authors believe in 'forward motion' as opposed to the traditional working-backward approach where we focus on our past incidents and mistakes to make better decisions in the future. With the realization that therapy should be about providing solutions and not just about talking about problems, the authors came up with five essential tools for success. These tools tackle very specific problems that are faced by almost all of us at various points in our lives. The tools are about connecting you to a higher force and letting that power work through you by applying the tools.

Chapter Analysis

Chapter 1: Revelation of a New Way

In a Nutshell

In this chapter, a young therapist named Michels met a patient who was worried that her boyfriend might be cheating on her. He tried to help by talking about her past, but it didn't work. Frustrated with this approach, Michels found someone named Stutz who had a better way to help people. Stutz's method involved using practical tools to solve problems and believing in something like a superpower inside us.

Roberta's Story

As a young psychotherapist, Michels met with a patient named Roberta who had a very specific request. She was obsessing over the idea that her boyfriend was cheating on her and wanted a clear method to stop it. Michels took the route his education and training told him to take: dive deeply into her childhood issues. Surprisingly, **she already knew what caused her problems**. Her father left her family when she was a child, and this caused her to fear abandonment, which by extension caused her to worry that her boyfriend would cheat and leave.

Because she already understood her issue, Michels' advice was useless. Finding the root of issues is all he learned and trained for. He **did not have a clear method to stop her obsessive behavior**. When he brought this up to two of his supervisors, all they said was 'go deeper,' which still did not give him a method of solving the issue at hand.

This lack of a solution bothered him. Psychotherapists, he now saw, could not solve a problem, they could only look at the past and try to figure out what caused it. Michels then set a path to look for answers himself and found Stutz, a doctor who was revolutionizing the industry with his **methods of focusing on the solution and not the problem.**

Solution-Oriented Methods of Therapy

Stutz was delivering a series of seminars on his new-found solution-oriented methods of therapy. He believed that **every human being possesses an untapped 'higher force'** that would enable him to solve his problems using certain 'tools.'

Stutz stumbled upon a young surgical resident named Tony who felt extreme anxiety about the board certification exams. Going **the traditional way, Stutz went deep into his past** and found the root cause to be his father who had feelings of inferiority and feared his surgical resident son would surpass him. Tony believed that if he passed the test, his father would retaliate, damaging their relationship.

Stutz advised that if he kept talking about the problem, his anxiety would go away, and he would pass his exam; Stutz was wrong. Tony failed miserably. He accused Stutz of not truly helping, as he never gave a solid solution to tackle his problem but rather simply thought it would go away if they talked about it continuously. This led to **the discovery**

of the solution-oriented approach that would give people the power to fight back.

With the loss of his brother to cancer at 12 years old, Stutz basically became his father's therapist, but he never seemed to recover from the loss of his son. Stutz's personal experience caused him to pursue psychiatry. With experience, he **focused on his patients' present rather than the past**. He recognized that dwelling on the past did no good. Instead, solving it 'then and there' is what matters.

The 'Tools'

The 'tools' he designed are practical behaviors and not mere attitude adjustments. An attitude adjustment is useless if not put into action. **The 'tools' are specific procedures** that control behavior to combat a specific problem. When people put the tools to work, it connects their minds to a world of infinite forces that aid in solving the problem.

Stutz focused on two terms: 'higher forces' and 'higher world.' He discovered that people could **tap into their hidden unexpected power** in emergencies that require them to be more courageous and resourceful, but as soon as the emergency goes away, they lose this power. He taught his patients to tap into this power at will, whenever they needed to, handing them the power to change their lives.

For these unseen forces to unravel their potential, you need **faith.** Humans have an absurd nature of quitting things that work for them. It is absolutely necessary to fight the resistance and continue applying these tools.

Faith will let you accept that these higher forces are real and that the tools enable the higher forces to come *through* oneself from the higher world. It is important to note that when one awakens the higher forces, it will benefit everyone around them.

Key Points

- Michels was taken aback when he realized how far-fetched psychotherapy is in solving real-life problems that his patients have. He was only trained to dig deeply into the past and find the root cause but nothing beyond it.

- Stutz was a psychiatrist who faced the same issue and was establishing a set of tools that would help solve his patients' problems.

- The tools are practical behaviors, that encourage action rather than attitude adjustments.

- The tools connect with a higher power to work through you, and you need faith to let it work.

Reflective Questions

1. Do you feel like you are ready to act toward solving your problems?

_____

_____

_____

_____

_____

2. Are you open to learning these tools that will enable you to solve your problems effectively?

_____

_____

_____

_____

_____

3. Are you ready to have faith in the tools and let them work their magic?

_____

_____

_____

_____

_____

Action Plan

1. Identify a set of problems that have been bothering you lately.

_____

_____

_____

_____

_____

2. List down the most prominent reasons why they arose. What are you doing or not doing that is causing these problems?

_____

_____

_____

_____

_____

3. Come up with a set of solutions.

_____

_____

_____

_____

_____

4. As you learn the tools in the next chapters, try to apply them to find solutions.

_____

_____

_____

_____

_____

Chapter 2: The Tool: The Reversal of Desire, The Higher Force: The Force of Forward Motion

In a Nutshell

In this chapter, we learn about how people often prefer instant pleasure and avoid discomfort. Stutz introduces the concept of the "Force of Forward Motion," which empowers people to face discomfort and move toward their goals. A key tool is the "Reversal of Desire," where you embrace discomfort and act courageously in the present to achieve a better future. This approach helps you overcome fears, expand your horizons, and find your inner strength.

Vinny's Story

This chapter looks at how **humans yearn for instant gratification** and how the reversal of this desire can enable them to keep moving forward in life. Michels once had a thirty-three-year-old patient named Vinny who alienated people using his wit and sarcasm, forcing them to instantly dislike him. Vinny was a talented stand-up comic, performing at small bars, events, and comedy clubs. His manager tried countless times to sign him up for bigger events, talk shows, and high-end charity events, but Vinny always shot them down. He gave disappointing excuses such as "he wasn't a morning person" when he needed to wake up for an audition, or "he didn't want to be at the mercy of big entertainment companies," etc.

This pattern was disturbing for his manager and hence Vinny was pushed to go get psychological help, which brought him to Michels. After having a long conversation, Michels found out that Vinny had an abusive father who beat him whenever he performed his acts. As a kid, he loved performing in front of crowds, but as the beating got harder, he gave up on his dreams. He developed a fear of it. He stayed in his comfort zone of performing for smaller crowds and never gave anyone a chance to inflict pain on him ever again. However, this was costing him his career, as **he was giving up on his dreams to avoid potential pain**.

Pain as Opportunity for Growth

It is natural to want to avoid pain, and **most people tend to never step beyond the invisible wall** they've created for themselves. They enjoy staying in their comfort zone, as it keeps them safe; it becomes a way of life. Vinny's comfort zone was small clubs, a small circle of friends who laughed at his jokes, a girlfriend who never expected much of him, etc. These were not pushing him to reach his full potential.

When you decide to step out, the first thing you will face is pain, but **beyond this pain lies endless opportunities**. When people cannot get past the pain, they become comfortable avoiding pain, and they insist on replacing the pain with pleasure. They look for instant gratification and get addicted to internet surfing, watching movies, pornography, comfort food, online shopping, gambling, etc. The important thing to understand is that these will entertain you for only a limited amount of time. Once it is over, reality strikes, and you will realize your sense of purpose in life is withering away. The comfort zone will keep your life safe, but it will also keep your life small.

The Higher Force – The Forward Motion

People with a sense of purpose do not think twice about enduring pain in the present to get to where they need to be in the future. You will not experience a sense of purpose just by thinking about it. You need to start **acting toward the future you need**. The moment you take action, you activate a higher force that enables you to forget about the pain and move forward. This is the Force of Forward Motion. This force goes hand in hand with the universe itself.

From microorganisms to entire species, the world has been constantly evolving without stop. Thinking like this similarly will help you endure pain in the present and pick yourself up from any disadvantageous situation. The force only works if you choose to use it consciously. You also need to accept the pain that comes with it. Most of us choose to avoid the pain and wallow in sadness, not live life to our highest potential. However, if you start taking action, you will **match the energy of the force and it will start doing wonders *through* you**.

The Tool – Reversal of Desire

Now that you know you need to tap into a higher force, you need to **reverse the desire of staying in your comfort zone**. You need to face pain fiercely. There are three steps to this process. Say,

1. "Bring it on!"

2. "I love pain."

3. "Pain sets me free."

In a three-step process, you first walk straight into pain. Secondly, you keep moving forward through the pain. Finally, you feel a state of achievement and bliss. **If you master the worst, you need not fear anything else**, and now you desire to face it rather than avoid it.

Pain is not absolute. It all depends on how you see pain and react to it. If you go straight at it, it shrinks. Moving away will only make it grow. If you avoid it, it will follow you. You must face it. The tool will let you know when to use it and these are called 'cues.' The **cues are easily recognizable moments**.

1. Cue 1 – Use the tool just before you are about to do an activity you want to avoid. It could be making a phone call, setting up an interview, finishing a project, etc. When you feel the pain creep in, do not stop to think, just do it! Take action.

2. Cue 2 – Whenever you start *thinking* about a dreaded task in the future, use the tool. It's all about training your mind to use the tool *right now*.

The Tool in Action – Michel's Story

The tool has proven that once you start making moves, opportunities flow endlessly. Until you make that move, nothing goes your way. **The universe helps those who help themselves.**

Michels was missing his sense of purpose working as a lawyer, but it was his comfort zone. He earned a good salary and going to school for psychotherapy for another four years meant he would have to leave his full-time job at the law firm. He sent out resumes to many law firms asking for part-time work so he could support himself during school. All of them turned him down except one. **The higher force opened doors once Michels began working for it.**

Forward Motion for Development

Similarly, if you activated the forward motion, it puts you in sync with the motion of the universe, bringing you tremendous opportunities. It is wise to accept that the universe has plans for you that do not include outer indicators of success, such as a house, car, or career. It cares about who you are inside and works on **developing your inner strengths**.

This is why, one after the other, the universe never stops sending adversity toward us. It develops your inner strength. Every human has a hidden inner strength that only comes out during adversity. **The tool enables you to tap into this strength at your will**, not just during adversity. Behaving like a victim and complaining, does not get you anywhere. The faster you accept *what is* rather than *what should be*, you will find it easier to pursue a solution.

Forward Motion for Power

This strength you develop will give you the **power to face anything** life throws at you. A famous Austrian psychiatrist named Victor Frankl was enslaved in four Nazi camps and lost his parents, brother, and wife. No matter what he endured – starvation, sleeplessness, threat of death, etc. – there was one thing the Nazis could never take away from him: his will.

He preached that life is about finding out what life expects out of you and **rising to the challenge**. If you and life have conflicting expectations, life will win. Ultimately, you will have to become selfless and dedicate your life to a higher force to work wonders through you.

Forward Motion for Courage

This inner strength also develops **courage**. Courage is the ability to act when faced with fear. Fear is almost always linked to a terrible future event that we feel might happen. Fixating on this future image will paralyze you if you let it. It will stop you from doing what you love until you are certain nothing will harm you.

This kind of certainty is impossible to achieve, however. It is more like an illusion of future certainty. If you give up this fear of the unknown, it will **free you to focus on the present**, which is the only place you can act. You need to understand that the event is in the future, but the fear you have is in the present. Fear is a certain type of pain as well, so you can use the tool of reversal of desire to overcome it.

As you practice, you will be able to overcome any fear, no matter what you're afraid of. Train yourself to desire fear and take courageous action. Not thinking about the future and only of the fear will enable you to act with boldness in the present. Stutz explains this as 'the process of fighting your way back to the present.' Most people don't want to actively be in the present; they wander away in the glory days of the past or dream of the future, but **the only thing that matters is the present**.

Some facts to keep in mind are:

1. You might feel overwhelmed with all these tools and feel like it is a prolonged process. In reality, the tool takes less than three seconds to apply. Of course, it takes some effort in the beginning to train yourself to use these tools, but in the long run, they will help you a lot.

2. You cannot expect instant results. Like any other skill, it takes time to master. All that matters at the beginning is the right attitude to commit to the tool. With time, you will reap maximum benefits.

3. You may think you are inviting pain by saying 'I love pain,' but it is not so. You are simply saying you love the pain that a particular event that has already happened caused you. You are not inviting bad things to happen to you.

4. You may question why pain keeps happening to you. The sooner you realize that life will never stop introducing pain and discomfort, the better. Once you accept it, you will be able to focus on the real problem of coming up with a solution. The more pain you tolerate, the more you will learn.

5. It is not masochistic to desire pain. Pain comes in two forms: necessary pain and unnecessary pain. Necessary pain is inevitable. For example, if you are a performer, rejection and large crowds are

necessary pain. Unnecessary pain is the pain you inflict on yourself under your own control. For example, the pain of not realizing your full potential is something you can control by taking action.

6. If you are a person who thinks you have no fears or pain, you are probably just stuck in your comfort zone. You have chosen to not pay attention to anything beyond your comfort zone and hence deliberately ignore opportunities, telling yourself that you have no fears.

7. Moving forward does not mean hyperactivity. It does not mean you have to always keep your mind busy either. Always keeping your mind busy is really just a way of avoiding the real fears and pain in you. Forward motion is a tool to face these problems you are avoiding. Your mind can relax only by facing your fears, not by avoiding them.

Other Uses of Reversal of Desire:

1. It enables you to expand your professional circle, as you now are fearless in pursuing new jobs, relationships, and friend circles. It will give you the strength to approach people you never could before.

2. It enables you to wield authority. If you are in a position of authority, you face many fears, such as the fear of not being liked, the fear of making wrong decisions, the fear of letting your followers down, etc. Facing fear and focusing on the

problems at hand can inspire your followers to respect you.

3. It will help you overcome phobias that hold you back. The phobia of large crowds can be the worst enemy of a great performer. The tool will help you put yourself in situations you have avoided all your life to finally overcome them.

4. It enables you to develop the discipline to make long-term commitments. Commitment requires you to make small, continuous, and painful steps frequently. If there has been a long-lost talent of yours that you never dared to pursue, use this tool to find the time and courage.

5. It will give you a new perspective on family dynamics from childhood. Think of something that you have avoided since you were a child, such as a trauma you went through that made you avoid future situations like it at all costs. Now think how you would've tackled it if you used this tool during your childhood. Let it build up inner strength in you.

Key Points

- You avoid going out of your comfort zone as it keeps you safe, and outside of it gives you pain.

- If you want to live life to the fullest, you need to step out.

- The force of Forward Motion will enable you to keep moving forward despite the pain. It's about understanding that the world only moves forward, and you need to find your sense of purpose so that you will be willing to endure pain in the present for a better future.

- Use the tool 'Reversal of Desire' to welcome pain and deal with it head-on. Reverse your desire of avoiding pain.

- This tool will build power and courage in you to take on any challenge life throws at you.

- There are two instances you can use the tool. One, when you are about to do a task you hate, and two, whenever you start thinking of a task you hate that you need to do in the future.

Reflective Questions

1. Are you avoiding any task, project, or person that you do not like?

_____

_____

_____

_____

_____

2. What is keeping you from finishing that task or project?

_____

_____

_____

_____

_____

3. Can you name the fears that you are feeling?

_____

_____

_____

_____

_____

4. What is your comfort zone?

_____

_____

_____

_____

_____

5. Have you ever been able to come out of your comfort zone in the past? If yes, what did it feel like?

_____

_____

_____

_____

_____

Action Plan

1. Think of a task you are currently avoiding. Think of why you hate doing it; visualize the pain.

_____

_____

_____

_____

_____

2. Now, walk straight into the pain and say, "bring it on!"

_____

_____

_____

_____

_____

3. You will feel like turning back but think that you love enduring that pain.

_____

_____

_____

_____

_____

4. Now tell yourself that the pain sets you free as you have currently completed the ask you hate and you no longer must think about it.

_____

_____

_____

_____

_____

5. Repeat this whenever you encounter a dreaded situation.

Chapter 3: The Tool: Active Love, The Higher Force: Outflow

In a Nutshell

This chapter talks about how we often hold grudges and seek revenge when someone upsets us, which makes us feel bad. Amanda couldn't forgive her boyfriend for a small mistake, and this made her angry and unhappy. To feel better and move on, we should practice "Active Love," which is a way to let go of anger and choose happiness instead.

Amanda's Story

When someone angers us, sometimes we cannot get them out of our heads. We plot revenge, giving them more focus in our lives than they deserve. This **takes up more energy** than you would think, holding you back from focusing on better things. This chapter looks at using active love to avoid falling into this trap.

Amanda was an entrepreneur who owned a high-end clothing business. She insisted that her boyfriend, Blake, accompany her to all fashion events. Although he was extremely uninterested in these events, he attended them to show his support. At one of these events, he struck up a conversation with a saleswoman at the cosmetics counter.

Amanda felt humiliated and disrespected because she felt her boyfriend was making her look bad by flirting with another woman. When she confronted him, he explained how he hated these events but still went with her and had a good time for the first time by having an interesting conversation with the saleswoman. Amanda was furious and thought of ways to get back at him.

Her anger continued, and although Blake tried to make it up to her, she did not budge. She just could not forgive him. She **realized that this was a pattern**, something that she did with all her past relationships. It only took one mistake, and she could never forgive her partner again.

The Maze

Once you start heading towards this point of no return, you are **trapped in a maze of hurt** and vengeful feelings. Any relationship can have problems, but being stuck in an unforgiving state hurts the relationship more than the mistake itself. These feelings can be seen in any situation, not just in relationships.

A person cutting you off in traffic or a neighbor's loud music can make you have this reaction. It is called a maze because it keeps you trapped in a vengeful state that is very hard to escape from. You become obsessed with the person who wronged you, giving them more time and energy in your life. **Once you're in the maze, it only damages you** and does nothing to the other person. You start seeing only the bad in them, forgetting all the good. Being stuck in the maze not only damages your present, but your future too.

As you fixate on the past wrongs that have been done to you, **life passes you by** and you will turn your back on your future. The most frustrating thing about the maze is that although you can see the damage it is doing to you, you may still find it impossible to escape. You become your own worst enemy.

The Higher Force – Outflow

The reason we become trapped in the maze is that we believe in **universal fairness**. We expect that life should treat us fairly, so we plot futile attempts to get revenge and restore fairness in the world.

To stop this, you need to practice a form of **love that is independent of your immediate reactions** to wrongdoing. This form of love is known as 'Outflow.' It is an *infinite, spiritual force that gives itself without restraint*. This takes away the power from the person who wronged you and gives it to yourself. Now, only you are in control of your feelings and emotions. You no longer let anyone else have control over you.

The Tool – Active Love

Active Love is the **love given out through conscious effort** to someone who has wronged you. Of course, you don't feel like loving someone who hurt you, and that is why you need to put conscious effort into it. It's a combination of effort and love. There are 3 steps to this tool.

1. **Concentration** – Gather all the love surrounding you and concentrate it in your heart. Think about a warm liquid light that is infinitely loving. Imagine that your heart is filled with it.

2. **Transmission** – Transmit all the love to the person who wronged you.

3. **Penetration** – Feel the love enter them. This will make you one with them and help you accept injustice, which will in turn help you move on.

Remember that **you always have a choice** when someone wrongs you. You can choose to be stuck in the maze or give active love and move on. Choose wisely. Some cues let you identify situations to use this tool.

1. Cue 1 – When you feel anger. Whenever you feel anger creeping in after someone wrongs you, use the tool.

2. Cue 2 – When you're reacting to a past memory of wrongdoing. This memory could be weeks or years old. You should not let such instances in the past put you in the maze.

3. Cue 3 – When you must deal with difficult people. Rather than worrying about how they will treat you, give them Active Love.

The Value of Active Love for Yourself

Loving a person who wronged you shouldn't be done because it's the 'right thing to do.' Whenever you're wronged, the last thing that comes to your mind is doing the right thing. Rather, this active love should be given because it is in **your own self-interest**.

You are hurting yourself if you continue to be in a state of rage. Whenever you use the tool, imagine the other person without a face. All your vengeful thoughts are attached to a face, so if you want to be able to send infinite love, imagine only that person's body and aim the outflow towards them. The beauty of outflow is that once you give it, **you will end up with more than what you had before**.

Some important facts to note:

1. You might feel that this tool enables others to get away with disrespecting you. Note that when you are enraged, you do not command respect. Therefore if you confront someone who wronged you while in a vengeful state, that confrontation brings nothing good. Conveying hate means that the relationship means nothing to you, and you are willing to destroy it. Rather, use the tool to realize there is some good left in the relationship.

2. It might seem fake to love someone you hate; however, you may not truly hate this person. One single incident is not worth getting so worked up over. This tool will help reshape relationships positively, as you now have the ability to take a moment before you voice your temporary emotions.

3. It can be difficult to imagine the amount of love needs to accomplish step one: 'Concentration'. If you have trouble, imagine you have a strong need or vulnerability in your heart. Once you direct it to the higher world of love, you will feel it.

Other Uses of Active Love

1. It builds self-control. A bad temper only brings trouble. The tool helps you control your anger.

2. It lets you be more assertive. If you let the anger build up, your confrontations will be dangerous, and people will not take you seriously. Using the tool, you can confront any situation calmly, commanding respect.

3. It trains you to accept others as they are. Fixating on past mistakes destroys the future. Rather than being mad and trying to change others, you can now accept them and move on.

Key Points

- When someone wrongs you and you keep thinking about avenging them, you get stuck in a maze. You stay trapped because you feel like you cannot think past their mistakes.

- We believe in universal fairness and assume that those who have wronged us should pay for what they did.

- Such vengeful thoughts do no good. You need to enable the higher force of 'Outflow,' which is a form of love, to be independent of your immediate reactions.

- Use the tool of 'Active Love,' which is love given through conscious effort.

- The tool comes in handy whenever you feel anger for something a person did to you, when you think of a memory of wrongdoing, or even when you must deal with difficult people.

Reflective Questions

1. Have you ever felt an exceeding amount of irritation or rage at your wrongdoers? It could be even the slightest trigger such as cutting you in traffic or walking slowly in front of you.

_____

_____

_____

_____

_____

2. What have you felt like doing to get revenge?

_____

_____

_____

_____

_____

3. Have you caught yourself dwelling in thought on
   such a person for prolonged amounts of time?

_____

_____

_____

_____

_____

4. How difficult do you think showing love to
   someone you dislike is?

_____

_____

_____

_____

_____

Action Plan

1. Think of a situation someone wronged you. You will
   feel the rage build up.

_____

_____

_____

_____

_____

2. Next, deviate your mind to think of all the love that surrounds you. Feel it penetrate your heart.

_____

_____

_____

_____

_____

3. Now, transmit all that love to your wrongdoer.

_____

_____

_____

_____

_____

4. Feel that love penetrate them. Visualize your love enter them and try to be one with them.

_____

_____

_____

_____

_____

5. Accept the situation and move on with your life as it is not worth dwelling upon.

_____

_____

Chapter 4: The Tool: Inner Authority, The Higher Force: The Force of Self-Expression

In a Nutshell

This chapter is about how people often feel insecure and have trouble connecting with others, like Jennifer, who wanted to fit into a social group but found it hard to talk to people. The book talks about the "shadow," which is the part of you that you're afraid of but need to accept. It also mentions the "Force of Self-Expression," which is about being yourself without worrying about others' opinions, and the "Inner Authority" tool that helps you gain control over your insecurities and connect with people more genuinely.

Jennifer's Story

Jennifer, a fashion model and single mother, was very keen on getting her ten-year-old son admitted into an elite soccer club. She pulled every string possible and spoke to sports journalists and anyone else who had a say in her son's admittance. Jennifer put in this effort because **she wanted to be accepted** into a social circle that she felt she could never join.

Jennifer's small-town background made her feel insecure in her current environment. She was overjoyed at the news of her son being admitted into the club, but it was short-lived. She still felt like an outsider among the parents, who she thought gave her strange looks and talked behind her back. She wanted to introduce herself and become friends with the mothers, but **every time she tried to speak, she froze**.

Freezing

This 'freezing' happens to everyone at one time or another. It often happens in front of an audience. Here, audience does not necessarily mean a crowd; it can also be one person whose opinion really matters to you. **Freezing is caused by an inner insecurity** that rips away your ability to connect with people.

Once Jennifer gathered some courage to speak to the other soccer moms, she found out that they were feeling insecure to talk to her because she was pretty and kept her distance from everyone. Jennifer realized **she had become self-obsessed over nothing**.

Connecting with people is vital, as those connections open up more opportunities than your talent or skills ever could. It is very difficult to overcome insecurities though. Many people turn to other things to avoid dealing with the underlying problem. For example, someone who finds it difficult to connect with people will do other things, such as lose weight, get an advanced degree, etc. rather than facing their fears. However, these activities do not provide a final solution. The tool discussed in this chapter will help you overcome these barriers.

The Shadow

Your **shadow is everything you don't want to be but fear you are**. Like your real shadow, it follows you everywhere you go. Imagine a situation when you felt insecure. Now take all those emotions and push them out and give them a face and body; that is your shadow. Your shadow determines how you see yourself.

In Jennifer's case, everyone else saw her as a good-looking model, but she saw herself as a social reject. Whenever we look at our *inner self,* we tend to be ashamed and look elsewhere for approval and validation. You need to understand that **no amount of approval will make your shadow vanish or make you feel worthy**; it should come from within. If you let others' opinions matter, you give them power over you to define your value. This chapter will help you bring this shadow out of hiding and become one with it.

The Higher Force – Self-Expression

Little kids are the best inspiration here. They are never afraid to express themselves, and they are devoid of all insecurities. They hardly ever freeze. They are filled with the 'Force of Self-Expression.' This allows them to **bring out the true self** within themselves with no care for anyone else's opinions.

As adults, we cower behind our outer selves, failing to express our genuine selves. You need to let yourself be the conduit between a higher force and yourself. We have turned our beautiful inner self into something we are ashamed of, the Shadow. **We need to learn to speak *through* the shadow**. That's where the below tool comes in handy.

The Tool – Inner Authority

Inner Authority is the authority you get over yourself by not letting anyone outside have it have power over you. To use this tool, you need to follow three steps:

1. **Visualize** your shadow – It could be your acne-faced thirteen-year-old self or the fear of becoming a narcissist like one of your parents. Take time and picture it.

2. **Bond** with it – Although you don't want to see this shadow image of yourself, you need to be able to develop a bond with it. Become one with it.

3. **Command** the audience to listen – Now, you and the shadow both turn to the audience and silently command them to listen. The audience will become smaller and smaller.

Here are some situations you can use this tool:

1. Cue 1 – Whenever you feel performance anxiety. Performance isn't about putting up an act. It can be any situation you are subject to judgment by others.

2. Cue 2 – An uncomfortable confrontation or request for help. Use the tool to connect with the other party so that the problem can be solved peacefully.

Self-Expression for a Unified Existence

As humans, we have a natural tendency to want to please others and expect validation in return. The best way to break away from this habit is to replace it with inner authority. The force of **self-expression lets you be you**.

You will feel your unique self as never before. It will bring you into harmony with the universe. This will make you experience yourself as part of a community, because now people respect you and consider you as one of their own.

As the shadow is every human's true self, you will all be speaking the same language: the language of the heart. This is how **different people can coexist in unity,** as they do not portray their fake personas. If you've noticed, children see no difference in race, creed, or color. That is because they speak the language of the heart. The inner authority also becomes a positive force for people around you. Leaders with insecurities tend to lead by coercion, but this tool teaches you to connect with people and gain their respect. Once everyone starts activating their inner authority, they will experience a 'social matrix' where interconnected people bring healing energy.

Some facts to note:

1. It's completely fine to not be able to see your shadow the first few attempts. It will come with practice. If you can't visualize it, try to feel it.

2. You will develop the ability to see your shadow while your eyes are open and even during a conversation.

3. Visualizing your shadow does not mean your mind will wander into another world. Rather, it will help you connect with the audience and stay in the moment.

4. You will not develop a split personality by visualizing your shadow. It is vital that you identify

your inner self to ensure you are realizing your fullest potential.

5. You might feel like your shadow is a part of your life that you want to avoid, however, avoiding it will not help you overcome your insecurities. Once you become one with it, your shadow changes. It becomes your partner in self-expression, creating an ongoing relationship.

6. We all have two types of shadows. This chapter looks at the 'inferior shadow,' but you might experience an 'evil shadow' too, which is when you see yourself acting out of pure self-interest with no regard for others. This tool helps you use the shadow the same way as discussed for the inferior shadow.

Other uses of inner authority:

1. You overcome initial shyness in developing romantic relationships. You no longer will freeze when you are approached by someone you like.

2. It lets you express needs and vulnerability. This is especially useful for men, as they tend to hide behind a façade of pride and ego, completely forgetting their inner vulnerable selves.

3. It lets you emotionally connect with loved ones. When you do not communicate with emotion, your loved ones may sense the distance between you.

4. It encourages self-expression through writing, not just speaking. Having the ability to tap into your

shadow will awaken your inner thoughts that when put on paper will let many people connect to you through it.

Key Points

- Your deepest insecurities turn into your shadow and keep following you unless you confront them.

- You are afraid of your inner self and hence look for validation from the outside. You let them define you and give them power over you.

- The higher force of self-expression enables you to freely express your inner self with no fear or regret.

- Use the tool 'Inner Authority' to become one with your shadow so that you are the only person in control.

- Use this whenever you are in a situation where you can be judged.

Reflective Questions

1. Have you ever identified all your insecurities?

_____
_____
_____
_____
_____

2. Do you remember a time you looked for external validation?

_____

_____

_____

_____

_____

3. What kind of thoughts do you have when you feel like you're being judged?

_____

_____

_____

_____

_____

4. Have you experienced a time when you freely expressed yourself and felt at peace?

_____

_____

_____

_____

_____

Action Plan

1. Think of a situation you had performance anxiety and froze.

_____

_____

_____

_____

_____

2. Think of all your insecurities, push them out of you, and give them a body and face. That is your shadow.

_____

_____

_____

_____

_____

3. Now feel a bond with it. Remember that it is a version of yourself.

_____

_____

_____

_____

_____

4. Together with your shadow, command the audience to listen. Visualize the audience becoming smaller and smaller.

_____

_____

_____

_____

_____

Chapter 5: The Tool: The Grateful Flow, The Higher Force: Gratefulness

In a Nutshell

This chapter discusses how constant worrying can create a "Black Cloud" of negativity, affecting your life and those around you. The author introduces the concept of "Gratefulness" as a higher force, connecting you to the Source, and presents the "Grateful Flow" tool to combat negative thoughts by actively practicing gratitude. The tool not only helps achieve peace of mind but also increases energy, motivation, and provides perspective, allowing you to accept success better.

Elizabeth's Story

Elizabeth was a successful guidance counselor at a community college and her husband was an awarded police officer. They had no imminent financial problems or other struggles, but she **always worried** about the littlest things. The problem was that these small things progressed to serious worries very fast.

For example, if she saw a new mole on her arm, her **chain of thought** would take her straight to cancer within moments. She then would go on to worry that she would die and think about how her family would survive without her. This habit was completely holding her back from living life to the fullest.

The Black Cloud

Elizabeth lived in a constant state of fear, **worrying about unrealistic problems**. She ignored every good thing around her and felt a huge weight on her shoulders, which was holding her back from living life freely. This is common for many people. We react to a world we've created in our minds which prevents us from seeing the world as it really is. The mind is powerful in that way.

The mind is able to create situations so believable that they become our reality. In a state of constant worry, it **generates so much negative energy** that everything starts to feel heavy. The weight blocks every positive emotion or situation from reaching you, making you feel like all that is left is doom. This heavy weight hanging over you is called a Black Cloud. Your negative thoughts take a life of their own, growing each day and holding you back.

The Black Cloud – Elizabeth's Story

The Black Cloud made Elizabeth feel like she was alone in this battle because no one else could see or feel how serious her worries were. It not only affected her, but it had begun **affecting her family** as well. Elizabeth's daughter considered her to be selfish at times, assuming her mom was nagging her just to satisfy her anxiety and not because she truly cared for her daughter. Elizabeth's husband stopped helping around the house because Elizabeth complained he wasn't doing anything right and said she would just do it herself. He felt useless and did not like being criticized all the time.

Finally, Elizabeth herself had not felt real joy in a long time. Because she was constantly worrying, she could not ever just sit down or relax. Ultimately, **she lost her peace of mind**. These were all the prices she paid for her negativity.

Trying to Control the Uncontrollable

Negative thoughts are difficult to let go of. They have so much more power compared to positive thoughts; it is very difficult to train our minds to switch from negative thoughts to positive ones. Worrying gives us a false sense of control. We do not like to believe that life takes its course, and so we try to control it on our own terms. The only way to do that is by worrying about future dangers (that may or may not happen) and taking measures to prevent them. This **lets us feel like we are in control** and ready for what life throws at us.

We assume that the universe is against us and is looking for every possible way to bring danger to us. Rather, **the universe *is* considerate** of our welfare. It provides us with food, air, water, and all things we need to live life to the fullest. The only way to feel the endless generosity of the universe is by being grateful.

The Higher Force – Gratefulness

Every day, we encounter incidents that could be life-or-death situations. We avoid car accidents, food poisoning, or illnesses, but **we never stop and think about being grateful** about it.

The power that endlessly gives is known as 'the Source.' It created you and continues to provide for you. Once you identify all that you have been given, you connect with the Source. It cannot be seen or heard, but **it can be felt through gratitude**.

The Tool – The Grateful Flow

Think of a situation where you felt deeply that something amazing had been given or shown to you, like a beautiful sunset or a starry night. You realize **something bigger than you created it**. Many of us have felt this way, but we rarely re-create it consciously. The only way to re-create it is to activate gratefulness at will. Here is what you can do to practice:

1. Think of five things that you are grateful for. It could be simple things such as being thankful for your eyesight, the hot water, your health, etc.

2. As you keep listing things, you will begin to feel a certain energy that does not need words. This energy is the Grateful Flow.

3. Feel the connection you made with the Source as this energy emanates from your heart.

Make sure you **name different items** that you are grateful for every time you use this tool. It will ensure you continue to feel how blessed you are and that will enable you to be grateful and connect to the Source. Here are some cues to use the tool:

1. Cue 1 – Use it immediately when you have negative thoughts, as any delay can push you into the Black Cloud very fast. Negative thoughts don't just mean worrying; they can include self-criticism, the judgment of others, or complaining.

2. Cue 2 – Use it at a specific time, such as the early morning or right before bed.

3. Cue 3 – Use it at times when your mind is undirected, such as during a train ride, when you're standing in line for coffee, when you're on hold during a phone call, etc.

This tool simply helps you to become the master of your mind. **The only thing a human can really control is their mind**, although we like to believe we control our lives.

Benefits of Grateful Flow: Peace of Mind

There are many benefits that come from using this tool. First, you will achieve peace of mind. We live in a constant state of unknowns. Anything could happen to us at any time, and we would never see it coming. It is useless to constantly worry about the unknown; it would be **more useful if you accepted this reality**.

You might feel like more money, more awards, or more material possessions would give you peace of mind, but the feelings brought about by these outward markers of success and achievement are short-lived. **True peace comes from being one with the Source**. You must keep connecting with the Source, therefore the idea of 'peace of mind' is an active state rather than a resting state. Our minds are wired to continuously think or worry about something, so to stop it you need to actively practice 'peace of mind.'

Benefits of Grateful Flow: Motivation

Second, this tool **increases our energy and motivates** us. Usually, we are motivated to acquire things we don't have, such as money, fame, status, relationships, etc. Our minds recognize the lack of something as the motivator.

However, once we gain these things, we quickly become dissatisfied and move on to the next thing. The sense of something missing could never connect you to the Source, but gratitude does.

Benefits of Grateful Flow: Perspective

Finally, Grateful Flow also enables us to gain perspective. Perspective is what **helps us move on from obstacles as we strive to see the bigger *positive* picture**. The Source provides awareness to recover quickly and get back on your feet and allows you to keep moving forward. It also enables you to accept success better.

Success is sometimes paralyzing because once you feel like you have achieved everything, you can become **afraid to take any more risks** that would tarnish your reputation. Therefore, many choose to think about past achievements rather than working on other areas of their lives. They stay safe in their comfort zone, no longer developing creative new ideas or projects. By using Grateful Flow, you acknowledge the hand of the Source in all your achievements and remain humble.

Some points to note:

1. It may take a considerable amount of time to feel the Source. Practice gratefulness by remembering five items you are grateful for, then be patient; you will discover the feeling with time and practice.

2. Being grateful does not mean ignoring your problems. It simply enables you to stop worrying and move on to constructive planning that would solve your problem. The Grateful Flow does not

ignore the darkness but rather helps you see the light amid your problems.

3. You might feel that gratefulness makes you lazy. You may crave the adrenaline rush given by worry. However, this adrenaline rush is finite physical energy. In a few moments, you will feel mentally exhausted. The only infinite mental energy flow comes from the Source.

4. Characterizing the Source as a human makes it feel closer to us. An intangible energy that *cares* seems a little far-fetched. Any organized religion personifies the divine in a way that enhances its connection to us, and the best way is to humanize it. The ultimate goal is simply to help you build a connection with it; how you personify it is irrelevant.

5. Believing the Source does not exist when adversity comes your way is natural. However, you need to understand that adversity is part of a bigger plan. The people who rise above adversity are the real winners. If adversity never hit them, they wouldn't have achieved what they have today. Adversity is simply a way the universe makes us realize our potential.

6. Worrying and trying to control the universe isn't a mark of a narcissist. A worrier simply does it to survive, not in expectation of praise.

7. The Source may be considered God. Different people have different religious beliefs and naming it God is up to you. For an atheist who experiences

Grateful Flow, his unconscious mind sees the world as all-giving, and that is all that matters.

Other uses of Grateful Flow:

1. It frees you from past regrets. Know that the world will only move forward and be grateful for what you have, believing that the Source will provide better things to you in the future.

2. It frees you from self-hatred. We all have a harsh inner voice that tells us we aren't good enough or are of no value. The Grateful Flow will help you see good things in yourself, letting you realize how blessed you are.

3. It stops you from being judgmental of others. Considering others to be inferior to you can damage your personal and work relationships. No one will want to be around you with that attitude. Once you become grateful for the people around you, you will be respected, valued, and loved.

Key Points

- If you are in a constant state of worry, you may feel like a huge weight is hovering over you, blocking good things from you. This is called the Black Cloud.

- The Black Cloud makes you focus only on the bad things in life.

- Practice gratefulness, as it is the higher force that will enable you to break through the cloud and bond with the Source, the giver of all things.

- Use the tool 'Grateful Flow' to feel grateful for the good things you have in life and stop worrying about the bad.

- You should use this tool as soon as you feel negative thoughts creeping in or as a habit at points throughout the day.

Reflective Questions

1. Do you worry about things a lot? Does it weigh you down?

_____
_____
_____
_____
_____

2. Do you feel like you have nothing good in life?

_____
_____
_____
_____
_____

3. What are the things you are grateful for right now?

_____
_____
_____

_____

_____

4. Do you feel like a huge burden has been lifted off
    your shoulders when you stop worrying?

_____

_____

_____

_____

_____

Action Plan

1. Think of 5 things that you are grateful for. Do this
    frequently, each time thinking of 5 different things.

_____

_____

_____

_____

_____

2. Feel the positive energy building around you. That
    is the Grateful Flow.

_____

_____

_____

_____

_____

3. Make a connection with the Source as it is the
    phenomenon that gives you all. Appreciate what it
    has given to you all this time.

_____
_____
_____
_____
_____

4. Use this repeatedly during the day or whenever
you feel negative thoughts.

_____
_____
_____
_____
_____

Chapter 6: The Tool: Jeopardy, The Higher Force: Willpower

In a Nutshell

This chapter highlights the common tendency to become complacent after achieving success. The higher force introduced is "Willpower," emphasizing the need for continuous self-improvement and staying connected to a higher force. The tool presented is "Jeopardy," encouraging a sense of urgency by visualizing the future at risk, transforming fear into willpower. This tool motivates individuals to act and become creators focused on adding value to the world, rather than mere consumers expecting rewards.

Vinny's Story Continued

Let's go back to Vinny from Chapter 2, a man who was afraid of being vulnerable in front of others and hence hid in small comedy clubs, completely disregarding his potential. With the use of Reversal of Desire, **he was able to land a part** in a major sitcom.

He then took his success for granted. He stopped using the tools and thought he didn't have to make any effort anymore. He indulged in beer, narcotics, and cheap adulation, completely dismissing the motivated person who worked on his skits every day, exercised, and cleaned his house. **He had recreated his comfort zone**, which quickly resulted in his doom. Within a few weeks, the sitcom manager had given him a final warning, as he was uncooperative, came to work drunk and late, and didn't get along with his co-stars. He also stopped therapy, spiraling downward and rendering all that effort useless.

Complacency

This is a common tendency for all of us, not just Vinny. **Once we get a taste of victory, we give up**. We believe there's nothing more to do.

Humans, however, are not finished products. We need to continuously keep working on ourselves. **We need to stay connected to a higher force** who will then continue to do wonders through us. This connection is not permanent. It will break in the face of adversity, and it is our duty to put effort to reconnect.

Adversity is never-ending, and this means that **the connection will keep breaking forever**. We keep looking for something magical that will make us complete. For Vinny, this 'magical something' was fame. Once he got it, he disconnected from the higher force which resulted in his doom.

Exoneration

We look for 'exoneration,' **the reward we expect to receive once we've used the tools and achieved what we wanted**. Exoneration means to be excused from a task or obligation. Deep down, we all want to be exonerated and to simply exist. However, the reality is often the opposite. We feel defeated when we cannot get this exoneration. The realization that life's struggles are endless will often demotivate us, and that is what stops us from continuing to use the tools.

There is a price you will have to pay for exoneration: demoralization. The more you feel exonerated, the more **you feel like you do not have to work anymore**. But then you realize you need to work even harder, and finally it will push you into a black pit where you are permanently demoralized and stop trying. This false hope of an 'easy street' is bound to shatter.

Consumerism

The enemy is 'consumerism.' We all become victims of it in one way or another. Every advertisement, billboard, or pamphlet wants us to buy something. They advertise products that are a must-have or will solve all your problems. This is a never-ending cycle as **once you buy a product you will use it for a few days and move on** to the next big thing.

Advertisements try to sell you a 'magical something' that has a higher force *inside* it. Before it can be of any use or as soon as it stops being of any use, you move on to the next thing, completely disregarding the fact that the real value is in **making a connection with a higher force *through* the product**. Take this book for example. If you read it in a consumeristic way simply to get some tools to make your life better, you might as well not read the book. The real value is in taking time to understand the tools and use them wisely in your life repeatedly.

The Higher Force – Willpower

Once demoralization has taken over you and you feel like you cannot move forward, your willpower is the only thing that can save you. In the previous four higher forces, they were defined as forces that are already present and gifted to us by the universe. Here, willpower solely depends on you. You need to **create it on your own**. Of course, you can consider it a higher force, however, you need to realize that you need to put effort into creating it.

Willpower is the spark that can be used to help you out of a difficult situation or when doing something you hate. This willpower is what will help you in continuing to use the tools even when you feel like you don't need them anymore. The difference it brings is that now you use the tools because you *want* to, not because you *have* to.

The Tool – Jeopardy

A sense of something being in 'jeopardy' is the tool **motivates urgency** in you. Many of us think we have all the time in the world and succumb to consumerism, wasting time on unnecessary cheap pleasures.

The best way to understand that you are putting your future in jeopardy is to visualize yourself on your deathbed. Death is often one of the best motivators, although it is unconventional to use this way. **It creates a sense of urgency like no other and creates a burst of energy** that will let you climb great heights.

We tend to limit our willpower to specific events, such as important exams, opening a business, closing a contract, etc. **We let our willpower fade** once the event is over. That does not work in the long run. You need a continuous source of jeopardy, and *that* is your future.

Try to visualize yourself in a few years if you never used the tools. You might see yourself unhappy, ill, poor, or living in disgusting conditions; all these are triggers for a future you are now putting in jeopardy if you do not work on yourself with the tools. Many of us fear we are wasting our lives, but we continue to bury ourselves with consumerism. However, **'jeopardy' helps us break through denial and transforms our fear into urgency** to act. That urgency then turns into willpower. Here are some cues for when to use 'jeopardy:'

1. Cue 1 – When you find it impossible to use the tools. You might feel lazy, exhausted, or just like giving up, use it.

2. Cue 2 – Whenever you feel like you no longer need to use the tool, use it.

3. Cue 3 – Whenever you lose the will to conquer important aspects in life, such as a new business, writing a new book, moving to a new city, etc. Use the tool.

Using this tool makes you become **a creator rather than a consumer**. Consumers expect the world to reward them for putting in little to no effort. They care only about getting rather than giving.

A creator does not think or act in this way. They are more focused on adding value to the world and being void of immediate gratification. Creative power cannot be given by God or anyone for that matter. It has to come from within you. And believe it or not, **life struggles are what truly bring out the creativity** in you. Humans are happiest when they have created something through effort; they are happiest when they realize their potential.

Some important points to note:

1. The very fact that we have no control over time makes 'jeopardy' a vital tool to be used. The sense of urgency it creates will ensure you take immediate action.

2. It is very easy to use 'jeopardy.' It takes less than five seconds to visualize yourself on your deathbed. That should be enough for you to be motivated to use this tool.

3. You might be against 'jeopardy' at first, as it seems like it is built on the fear of death. You are absolutely right. Fear is hardwired into our brains on a primitive level that guards our survival. 'Jeopardy' forces you to realize that your time here is limited.

Other uses of the tool:

1. It will give you the willpower to avoid addictive and impulsive behavior. We often cannot resist the need for immediate gratification. Jeopardy helps in avoiding such decisions.

2. It helps you concentrate in instances when you tend to daydream, succumbing to distractions. The fear of wasting your future away will always pull you back to earth and help you focus.

3. 'Jeopardy' enables you to start new ventures. The fear of the unknown is one of the most primal fears of mankind. Starting something new is always a challenge, and you are clueless about how it will turn out. Use this tool to overcome fear.

Key Points

- We keep looking for something that exonerates us, that frees us from having any responsibility.

- Being exonerated demoralizes us and prevents us from continuing to try. We fall prey to consumerism, as we keep consuming things that we believe will complete us.

- You will need the higher force of 'Willpower' to fight these urges off.

- Use the tool of 'Jeopardy,' as it will push you to live a life of no regret, establishing fear of jeopardizing your future.

- Use this tool whenever you feel like giving up and stopping the use of the tools.

Reflective Questions

1. Have you felt like stopping the use of the tools as you see no results?

_____
_____
_____
_____
_____

2. Has it demoralized you from doing what you want to and achieving your dreams?

_____
_____

_____

_____

_____

3. How would you feel if your life was full of regret on
    your deathbed?

_____

_____

_____

_____

_____

4. Will you be comfortable knowing you put your
    future in jeopardy since you did not take necessary
    action when it was needed?

_____

_____

_____

_____

_____

Action Plan

1. Visualize yourself on your deathbed. Examine if you
    see a life of regret or happiness.

_____

_____

_____

_____

_____

2. Now, understand that you are putting your future in jeopardy if you did not continue using the tools.

_____
_____
_____
_____
_____

3. Let the higher force of 'Willpower' take over. It is essential that you act on your negative feelings of demoralization.

_____
_____
_____
_____
_____

4. Use the tool 'Jeopardy' to ensure you keep practicing the tools so you can achieve your goals.

_____
_____
_____
_____
_____

Chapter 7: Faith in Higher Forces

In a Nutshell

This chapter explores the journey of Michels, who eventually believes in higher forces through personal experiences. Stutz introduces the concept of "spiritual evolution," where humans connect to the universe through a common source, the Force of Evolution. This force presents challenges, pushing individuals to evolve and become creators using the tools provided. Michels's transformation and Stutz's personal revelation highlight the importance of faith in a higher force, regardless of religious beliefs, emphasizing the power of connection for creative evolution.

Michels' Story

Because he was brought up in an atheist household, **Michels found it hard to believe in the higher forces**. When he first met Phil Stutz, he was utterly confused about the power of higher forces. Although Michels' patients found success with the tools and had faith in the higher power, Michels was unable to use the tools himself because his atheist background did not initially have room for such a belief.

As time passed though, he went through a series of events and experiences that made him think more about this higher power. He was focused on the tool of Active Love. He was fixated on feeling this love when his son was born on January 17th, 1992. One year later in 1993, he dreamed about an earthquake that shattered his office space, but during the dream, he experienced an enormous amount of love as he tried using the tool one last time before he died. Then in 1994, the costliest earthquake did occur, destroying his office exactly he saw in his dream. These events made him truly **wonder if a higher power exists**. He thought of all his past decisions – the decision to leave law, the decision to take up psychotherapy, the birth of his son, and then the dream. They were too good to be a coincidence. As a believer in rationalism, he could not understand this higher force.

Spiritual Evolution

When Michels talked to Stutz about it, Stutz explained that being confused is the beginning of new ideas. The **old ideas must be banished for new ones to enter**. Stutz went on to explain how we talk about 'physical evolution' regarding genetic advancement, but nobody talks about 'spiritual evolution.' 'Spiritual evolution' happens when all human beings connect to the universe through the same source and develop their inner self. This source is a certain spiritual system that we now define as a higher force.

When a human is faced with a problem, imagine that it is sent down by a higher force that governs evolution, **forcing us to evolve, get creative, and solve the problem**. Then, that human uses tools to solve that problem. The tools act as a set of upward steps, leading them to a better-evolved state, making them capable of doing things they never did before. They have become a creator.

The Force of Evolution

It is safe to say that both the problem and the higher force comes from the same source whose initial plan was to **make us evolve into advanced human beings**. This force is the Force of Evolution. This force cannot work unless you contribute your free will. You need to be willing to use the tools to climb up to that higher creative state.

Michels' Belief

Michels had to **put one of the tools into use to believe in it**. His best friend Steve was a renowned theoretical physicist who only believed in science. When he asked Michels to lunch to talk about work, Michels was petrified. He was afraid that he would be ridiculed by Steve for believing in higher forces that cannot be seen or touched. When he brought this up to Stutz, Stutz encouraged him to simply use Active Love with blind faith.

As he went into the lunch with Steve and spoke of the higher forces, Steve seemed to be on board with it. He mentioned that as long as a method works for people, it does not have to make sense. Michels felt relieved and stupid for caring about Steve's opinion so much. That is how **Michels became a believer** in the tools.

Stutz's Journey

Stutz also had to go through his own life incident to **believe in the higher force**. During his college years, he was learning about psychiatry and practicing it; he was full of energy and enthusiasm for his field.

However, with time, he felt an immense amount of exhaustion for no reason. His doctors prescribed many tests, but everything came back normal. They began to think it was all in Stutz's head. Since nobody could help him, he shut himself off from the outside world, which

forced him to look inward. He used this time deeply to think of the set of tools he now preached.

As he was struggling to create the tools, something clicked and information just started flowing from nowhere. He could not comprehend where it was coming from, but he knew **it was some kind of higher force that gave him access to the inner world** that had all the answers he needed. He felt the universe had plans for each of us and started to believe that it would teach us everything we needed to learn in our life.

It's all about faith. Though religion is not something either author practiced, they still had faith in a higher force that governs our life. Naming it and putting a face on it is up to the users of the force. What is important is **realizing the power of it and connecting with it** to become the creators that life intended.

Key Points

- The tools enforce an active relationship with higher forces. For people who do not believe in things they cannot see or measure, this can be a challenge.

- This book requires having faith in the tools. It may take time for them to work, but with practice, they will.

- If you cannot bring yourself to believe in the higher forces and tools, simply put them to use with no questions asked. See the results and decide for yourself if you want to use them.

Reflective Questions

1. Are you a believer in forces beyond what meets the eye?

    _____
    _____
    _____
    _____
    _____

2. Have you ever felt any such force work through you?

    _____
    _____
    _____
    _____
    _____

3. Are you willing to let yourself open to the higher forces?

    _____
    _____
    _____
    _____
    _____

4. Do you feel faith building up as you keep using the tools?

    _____
    _____
    _____

_____

_____

Action Plan

1. Pick a situation you can use one of the tools.

   _____

   _____

   _____

   _____

   _____

2. You may not believe in the power of the higher forces but have faith.

   _____

   _____

   _____

   _____

   _____

3. Use the tool in that situation and experience the results.

   _____

   _____

   _____

   _____

   _____

4. Keep at it as it may take some time to work.

   _____

   _____

   _____

_____

_____

5. Once you see results, you can start believing and
using them frequently.

_____

_____

_____

_____

_____

Chapter 8: The Fruits of a New Vision

In a Nutshell

In this chapter, the authors share three key ideas about a new way of thinking. First, they say it's important to experience higher forces rather than just thinking about them logically. Second, they highlight that everyone has the authority to decide their own spiritual beliefs, rejecting the idea of blindly following others. Third, they talk about how facing personal problems helps us grow and evolve. They also discuss using tools like Reversal of Desire, Active Love, Inner Authority, Grateful Flow, and Jeopardy to improve both individual and societal well-being. The authors emphasize the ongoing use of these tools for personal and collective growth.

The Pillars

The discovery by the two authors developed pillars of a new spirituality. This spirituality was **not built on blind faith but on patterns** that they both deduced.

Pillar 1 – It is worthless to simply keep thinking about the higher forces. You need to experience them.

Following the scientific method, we are trained to believe only in things we can prove logically. When Michels questioned Stutz about proving if the higher forces exist, Stutz simply told him to try the tools and experience the forces for himself. Accordingly, the higher forces' existence cannot be proved scientifically, it is **something that has to be experienced**. You need to stop thinking and simply apply the tools, which will guide you to the higher forces. You will begin to then have faith in them with time.

Pillar 2 – Each of us has our own authority in the face of spiritual reality.

In this new age, we are privileged to have the ability to come to our own conclusions based on our experiences rather than having to follow an authority figure, such as a priest, politician, monk, etc. We no longer are obligated to believe the Word of God blindly. The beauty of the higher forces is that it invites people to **experience them and then believe**. The new spirituality understands that each human is unique, and the higher forces affect them in unique ways at different times and places. Modern people like to choose their spiritual beliefs based on what's best for them. Although some may find this ignorant, it truly is empowering. The power to believe only lies within the people, not in any authority figure.

Pillar 3 – Personal problems drive the evolution of the individual.

We evolve when faced with our personal problems. Michels evolved when he had to confront Steve, and Stutz evolved through having an illness that no one could define. Similarly, when you face adversity, it pushes you to think, be creative and evolve. You feel better when you consider **adversity as a way of shaping your advancement** rather than considering it a setback. This is the fundamental difference between a consumer and a creator. A consumer who only expects to receive will not welcome adversities as they only looks to gratify their needs. A creator, on the other hand, welcomes adversities as he sees them as opportunities to grow. However, if we only grow as individuals and not as a society, we will never achieve our fullest evolutionary potential.

Healing a Sick Society

Modern society is so hung up on individual well-being that it has completely forgone the need to collectively develop as a society. We are dwelling on our past, unwilling to welcome new ideas and finding it difficult to connect with each other. The sooner we realize that society must move forward as the universe does, the better we will be able to become one with it. We need to transform from a society that is lacking faith and purpose to a **society that is engaging with higher forces** to reach its ultimate potential. Here is how we should use the tools to achieve it:

1. Reversal of Desire – As a society, we cannot stagnate in our comfort zone and be afraid to try new things. When everyone starts avoiding pain and starts moving forward, you can only assume that society will develop.

2. Active Love – Society is very risk-averse most of the time, shutting down people who bring in new ideas or simply anything different than the norm. If we all practiced Active Love and used the higher force of Outflow to embrace people in the face of disagreement or judgment, we would all be able to live in harmony.

3. Inner Authority – As individuals, we have a shadow, an image of ourselves that we never want to be. If we accept this inner part of ourselves, we will be able to project acceptance toward others and

express ourselves freely. A genuine, non-fake set of individuals who express themselves would bring unity to society.

4. Grateful Flow – Our society is filled with institutions and individuals who only think of themselves. This stems from their worry of never having enough. If everyone were grateful for what they have, especially the ones in authority, they would not try to rip people off. They would fulfill their duty to serve people as they should. Only a grateful society can counteract the selfishness that pulls people apart.

5. Jeopardy – As a society, we are waiting for something magical to happen that would free us from our tasks and obligations. We need to think about the future we are putting in jeopardy by not taking any measures to secure our society. If we could all visualize the person we are on our deathbeds, pondering what life could've been, we as a society will not put our future in jeopardy.

As the book comes to an end, it is vital to realize the importance of **using the tools continuously** in life. Put effort into maintaining a connection with the higher forces and realize your highest potential. Become a creator who gives back to the world. Only then will you experience true happiness.

Key Points

- The tools were created not simply by having blind faith but by identifying patterns in people.

- You need to experience the higher forces to truly believe in them. There is no use simply thinking about them.

- We have the authority to come to our own conclusions by experience. No one is forcing you to believe in the higher forces or tools.

- Individuals develop when faced with personal problems. Until adversity hits, humans will not develop nor become creators.

- We live in a sick society that needs to collectively use the tools to move forward.

Reflective Questions

1. Are you willing to let yourself experience the higher forces before you question them?

_____
_____
_____
_____
_____

2. Do you feel like you have the freedom to experience the higher forces and then arrive at a conclusion?

_____
_____
_____
_____
_____

3. Do you now believe in the higher forces working through you?

_____

_____

_____

_____

_____

4. Do you feel like you developed due to facing a certain adversity in your life?

_____

_____

_____

_____

_____

Action Plan

1. Once you understand the tools, prepare to put the tools into action. Simply thinking about them will not make a difference.

_____

_____

_____

_____

_____

2. Experience the work of the tools and conclude if you are a believer.

_____

_____

_____

_____

_____

3. Do not break in the face of adversity, rather use it as an opportunity to develop yourself. Become a creator not a consumer.

_____

_____

_____

_____

_____

Background Information about *The Tools*

The most common problem in psychotherapy or psychiatry that the authors identified was that they hardly gave solutions to people. People came to therapists for help, but it was unfortunate that none of the professionals had real solutions; the only thing they were trained to do is talk about the past and identify childhood traumas to get to the root cause of the problem. The authors realized that patients do not come to them to take a walk down memory lane. Most of them knew what was wrong with them. They needed solutions. This set Stutz on a path to discovering the five tools.

The problems outlined in this New York Times Bestseller are everyday problems that anyone can encounter, which makes them even more relatable. It gives very clear guidelines on what the tools are, what problems they address, what higher force it connects to, how to apply the tools, and how to continue to apply them throughout life. The book expects a level of practice from its readers. This book is not about giving knowledge but rather can be used as a guidebook or blueprint for action. To reap the true benefits, it is vital to apply the tools and experience the benefits for yourself.

The beauty of the tools is that they are proven methods for success. The authors wrote the book considered hundreds of their own patients' experiences, those who applied the tools and saw results. The authors do not force the reader to have blind faith in the tools. They invite the reader to see it for themselves, which is why this book truly complements modern society.

Background Information about Phil Stutz and Barry Michels

The two authors are known as the most sought-after shrinks in Hollywood, as their clientele ranges from actors, writers, and producers to CEOs and other distinguished individuals.

Phil Stutz is a graduate of the City College of New York and received his MD from New York University. He began his psychiatric training at Metropolitan Hospital where he started noticing the need for real solutions rather than simply talking about the problem. He then worked as a prison psychiatrist at Rikers Island and finally moved on to his private practice in New York City. Currently, he is practicing in Los Angeles where he moved in 1982.

Barry Michels received his Bachelor of Arts from Harvard University, his law degree from the University of California, Berkeley, and his Master's in Social Work from the University of Southern California. While practicing law, he had a change of heart and decided to pursue psychotherapy. Barry has been featured in many publications, such as The New Yorker and Time Magazine, and he has appeared on ABC's Nightline. His articles are published online on Psychology Today, Salon, and Quora. Michels has given numerous talks at In Good Health Summits, Google, the University Club of Chicago, the Writers' Guild, 20th Century Fox Television, etc. He now has a private practice in Los Angeles.

The authors have continuously researched other tools beyond the ones proposed in this book. On their website, thetoolsbook.com, there are a variety of tools, including tools for procrastination, tools for insecurity, tools for addiction, tools for conflict, and more. Each category gives very specific tools to overcome each obstacle. They have opened up a platform for conversation and discussion by connecting people with other psychology professionals through their website. Some of the celebrities that have used and praised the tools are actors Jonah Hill, Gwenyth Paltrow, Drew Barrymore, film director Adam McKay, and many others.

Trivia Questions about the Book

1.	What was the reason that Stutz began discovering the tools?

2.	What are the 5 tools discussed in this book?

3.	What is the name of the zone where people stay safe and never step beyond?

4.	What are the three steps of Reversal of Desire?

5.	What are the cues to use Reversal of Desire?

6.	What is the higher force related to the Reversal of Desire?

7.	Name 4 other uses of Reversal of Desire.

8.	Why is it so hard to get out of the Maze?

9.	What are the three steps of Active Love?

10.	Name 3 cues to use Active Love.

11.	How does Active Love build self-control?

12.	When and why do you freeze in front of an audience?

13.	What is the Shadow?

14.	Name the 3 steps of the Inner Authority tool.

15.	Name 4 uses of Inner Authority.

16.	Describe how the black cloud works.

17.	How can you let go of the black cloud?

18. What are you putting in jeopardy when you are demoralized?

19. What does the tool tell you to visualize when using it?

20. What is the name of the act of being free of tasks and obligations?

Discussion Questions

1. Do you feel is necessary to walk straight into pain to deal with it? Would you ever do it?

2. Have you ever been stuck in the Maze? Describe such a situation and what implications it had on you.

3. Do you feel like you can emanate active love for someone who has wronged you?

4. Do you think giving love to someone who has insulted you is stupid?

5. What does your Shadow look like? Do you feel like you can accept it and become one with it?

6. Do you believe in the Source? Do you think it is unintelligent to think that a higher source gives us everything rather than us achieving things on our own?

7. How do you think fate plays a role in this?

8. Think of an incident where you felt like you had a close save. Did you feel grateful for your life after it? What changes did you make in your life afterward?

9. Have you ever felt like you are wasting your life? What have you done in such instances?

More books from Smart Reads

Summary of the Case for Keto by Gary Taubes

Summary of Eat Smarter by Shawn Stevenson

Summary of 4 Hour Body by Tim Ferriss

Summary of Dr. Gundry's Diet Evolution by Dr. Steven Gundry

Summary of Exercised by David E. Lieberman

Summary of End Your Carb Confusion by Eric C. Westman with Amy Berger

Summary of Fast This Way by Dave Asprey

Summary of Dr. Kellyann's Bone Broth Diet by Dr. Kellyann Petrucci

Summary of Permission to Feel by Dr. Marc Brackett

Summary of Unwinding Anxiety by Judson Brewer

Summary of Set Boundaries, Find Peace by Nedra Glover Tawwab

Summary of The Complete Guide to Fasting by Jason Fung with Jimmy Moore

Summary of The Diabetes Code by Jason Fung

Summary of The Obesity Code by Jason Fung

Summary of A Radical Awakening by Dr. Shefali Tsabary

Summary of How to do the Work by Dr. Nicole LePera

Summary of COVID-19: The Great Reset by Steven E. Koonin

Summary of Unsettled: What Climate Science Tells Us, What It Doesn't, and Why It Matters by Steven E. Koonin

Summary of What Happened to You? by Oprah Winfrey and Dr. Bruce Perry

Summary of Breath: The New Science of a Lost Art By James Nestor

Thank You

Hope you've enjoyed your reading experience.

We here at Smart Reads will always strive to deliver to you the highest quality guides.

So I'd like to thank you for supporting us and reading until the very end.

Before you go, would you mind leaving us a review on Amazon?

It will mean a lot to us and support us creating high quality guides for you in the future.

Thanks once again!

Warmly yours,

The Smart Reads Team

Download Your Free Gift

As a way to say "Thank You" for being a fan of our series, I've included a free gift for you:

Brain Health: How to Nurture and Nourish Your Brain For Top Performance

Go to www.smart-reads.com to get your FREE book.

The Smart Reads Team

Made in the USA
Las Vegas, NV
03 January 2024

83878613R00056